PAPER MAGIC
The Art of
ORIGAMI

By Katherine Gleason   Illustrated by Meryl Henderson

Troll

Mark Dallas Butler, in memoriam (1961-1993)

−K.G.

To my husband, Jim.

−M.H.

The binding of this book is specially designed so
that you can pull out the patterned origami papers in the
middle. Remove these pages carefully. In addition, take
care not to break the spine of the book to avoid
loosening the instruction pages.

Welcome to the World of Origami

Origami, the art of paper folding, is an ancient art form. Origami is so old that no one is positive when it was invented or where. Some people believe that origami was born in China shortly after the invention of paper in the year 105. Other people think that the art of paper folding was developed in Japan in the sixth century. We do know that the word "origami" comes from the Japanese words for paper and for fold. "Ori" means fold and "gami" is a variation of the word "kami," which means paper.

Early origami enthusiasts had to be careful. Paper used to be handmade, so it cost a lot of money. After the invention of a paper-making machine in 1798, paper became cheaper and origami grew more popular in Europe and America, as well as in Japan.

Today origami is both a fun hobby and a respected art form. Children in Japan learn origami in school. Artists who create original origami figures exhibit their work in museums. All over the world, origami societies promote the fascinating art of paper folding. When you make figures with the papers included in this book, you'll be part of an ancient tradition that is still growing in popularity in the modern world.

THE FOLDS

The fold is one of the most important things to master when learning to make origami. Make all your folds as carefully as you can. Check that your fold is accurate, then use your thumbnail to make your creases sharp.

VALLEY FOLD
You will probably use the valley fold the most. It gets its name because after you make it, the paper seems to form a valley.

MOUNTAIN FOLD
The mountain fold is similar to the valley fold except it's upside down, and it gives the paper a mountain shape.

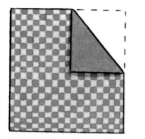

INSIDE REVERSE FOLD
This fold allows you to position a point between two layers of paper. Often it is used for the heads of birds and the feet of birds and animals.
1) Fold a piece of paper in half. Fold one corner down. Crease well.
2) Unfold the crease you just made and push the corner down between the two layers of paper. The corner will fold along the creases you made in Step 1 and will end up inside the two layers of paper.

OUTSIDE REVERSE FOLD

This fold is also used when making birds.
1) Fold a piece of paper in half diagonally.
Fold one point up. Crease well.

①

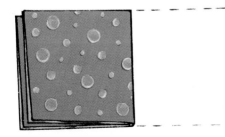

②

2) Unfold the point and let the paper open.
Hold one half of the creased corner in each
hand with your thumbs on the crease. Push
your thumbs down and pull the point up so
that the point turns inside out.

SQUASH FOLD

The squash fold is used when the paper has
already been folded. With this fold you get to
squash the paper into position.
1) Fold the paper in half.

①

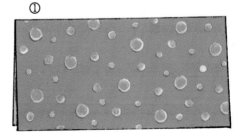

②

2) Fold the paper in half again. Crease
well and unfold.

THE FOLDS

3) Fold the corner down to meet the center line. Unfold. Put your fingers inside the half you just creased. Push the paper down so that the crease on the top triangle meets the folded edge inside the figure.

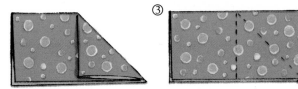

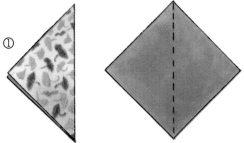

BLINTZ BASE
The blintz base gets its name from the tasty folded pancake that it resembles.

1) Fold the paper in half diagonally and unfold.

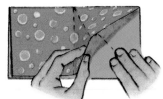

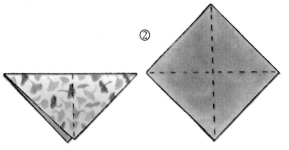

2) Fold the paper in half along the other diagonal and unfold.

3) Fold all four corners to meet at the center of the two creases, and your blintz base is complete!

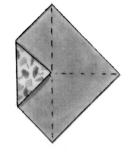

6

Always work on a clean table top. This will help you to make neat folds.

To help you get the angle of a fold, you can match your figure up with the drawing in the book. Even though the illustration is smaller than your figure, the angles are still the same.

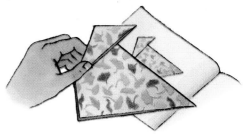

It's easier to fold the paper away from you. To fold the paper in half diagonally, hold the paper with your thumb and index finger on the outside of the fold and your other fingers on the inside. Pull the top corner away from you. Line the two corners up. Hold them in place with your index fingers and make the crease with your thumbs.

Besides making neat folds, the other important thing you'll need when making origami is patience. It's easier to stay patient if you start with the easy figures at the beginning of the book. After you can fold them, work your way up to the more complex ones.

If you find yourself getting frustrated, take a few deep breaths, shake out your hands, and roll your shoulders. Or take a short walk. Even walking around your work table can help. Sometimes taking a break from a project will let you see it in a whole new light. After you have mastered a tricky figure, not only will you have something to show your friends, but you'll feel great, too!

CUP

If you make this cup with white paper, you can use it to take a drink. The United States Air Force used to include directions for this cup in one of its training manuals. The book recommended that all members of flight crews learn to make this figure. With this knowledge and a page ripped from the manual, they would never be stranded without the means to take a drink.

1) Keep the side of the paper you want for the body of the cup on the outside. Valley fold the paper in half diagonally.

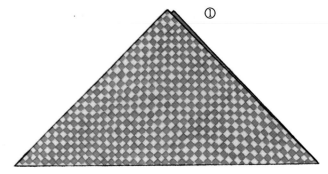

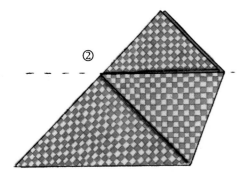

2) Valley fold the right point to meet the sloping left side of the figure. Make sure that the top edge of the point you are folding is parallel to the bottom of the figure.

3) Valley fold the left point so that it meets the top right corner.

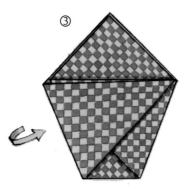

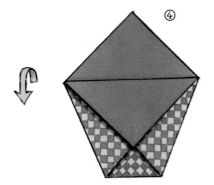

4) Valley fold the top layer of the top point down as far as it will go.

5) Turn the figure over and valley fold the top point down on this side, too. Squeeze the sides of the figure a little so it is not flat, and your cup is complete.

Here's another idea—make the cup with a square piece of paper that measures 22" x 22" (54 x 54 cm). When you are done, you can wear it as a hat.

SAMURAI HAT

Make big hats and wear them at parties. You can use smaller hats to dress up your stuffed animal friends.

1) Keep the color you want your hat to be on the outside. Valley fold the paper in half diagonally.

①

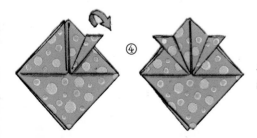

②

2) With the long side of the triangle away from you, valley fold the left and right points down to meet the corner near you.

3) Valley fold the top triangles in half so that the bottom points meet the far corner.

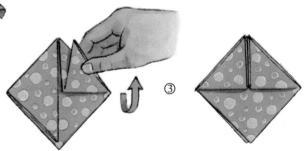

③

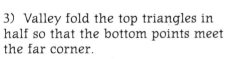

④

4) Valley fold the inside edges of the top triangles so that they stick out to make horns.

10

5) At least $\frac{1}{4}$ inch (.6 cm) from the center, valley fold the top layer of the bottom flap up so that the point meets the line between the horns. The point should fall below the tops of the horns.

⑤

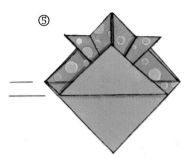

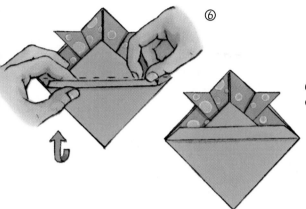

⑥

6) Valley fold the remaining $\frac{1}{4}$ inch (.6 cm) of the bottom flap at the center line.

7) Mountain fold the bottom layer of the bottom triangle at the center line. Open your hat up, and it is ready to wear.

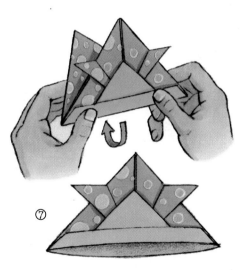

⑦

If you want to wear this hat, make one with a large piece of paper. Use a 20" x 20" (50 cm x 50 cm) square. If the hat is too big when it is done, fold the corners at the sides over to adjust the size.

11

PINWHEEL

Pinwheels are fun on windy days. Even if there is no breeze, you can blow on your pinwheel to make it turn.

1) Make a blintz base (see page 6). To do this, valley fold the paper in half diagonally. Unfold it and fold it again on the other diagonal. Unfold. Valley fold all four corners in to meet at the center.

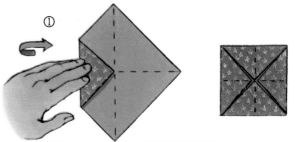

2) Unfold the flaps on the right and left sides so that the corners stick out. Turn the figure over and valley fold both corners so that they meet at the center point.

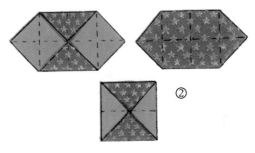

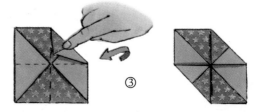

3) Valley fold the top right and bottom left corners to meet at the center.

4) Mountain fold the remaining two points to meet at the center on the other side of the figure. You might find this step easier to do if you turn the figure over and valley fold the remaining points to meet at the center. If you turned the figure over to do this step, remember to turn it back.

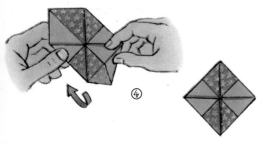

5) Look underneath the double layered top flaps that meet in the center. You will find two single layered flaps that also meet in the center. Grab the single layer flap on the right by the point. Hold the figure in the middle so that the double layer flaps stay in place. Pull the single layer flap down and to the right so that it folds along its center line. Crease the center line so the flap lies flat.

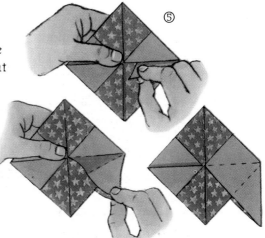

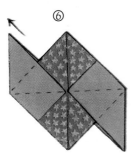

6) Pull the single layer flap on the left side of the figure up and to the left. Hold the double layer flap on the other side of the figure down while you complete this step.

7) Turn the figure over. Pull the two remaining single flaps out. Use a tack to attach your pinwheel to a pencil eraser, and you're ready to catch the wind!

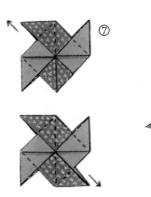

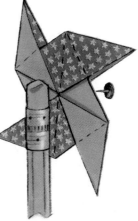

FORTUNE TELLER

You can use this figure as a fortune teller or as a container for small objects.

1) Make a blintz base (see page 6). Turn the figure over.

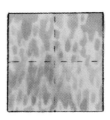 ①

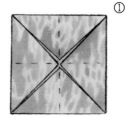

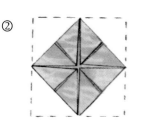 ②

2) Fold all four corners in to meet in the center.

3) Fold the figure in half, crease, and unfold. Fold the figure in half the other way. Crease and unfold.

 ③

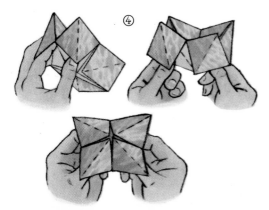 ④

4) Slide the thumb and index finger of your left hand into two of the pockets on the underside of the figure. Put the thumb and index of your right hand into the remaining pockets. Push the four fingers together and the figure is ready for you to add fortunes. Or turn the figure upside down and you have a candy dish or a paper-clip holder.

To add fortunes, write a number on each of the four outside flaps. Write the name of a color on each of the eight inside panels. Open up each point on the inside and write one fortune on each of the eight sections. Fold the flaps back down and you are ready to tell fortunes.

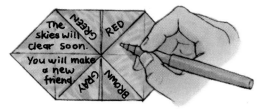

To tell a fortune, hold the fortune teller with the thumb and index fingers of both hands as in Step 4. Keep your fingers together so that the mouth of the fortune teller remains closed. Ask the person whose fortune you are telling to pick a number from the outside flaps. Count out the number that the person picked by opening the mouth. First open the mouth one way. Then open it the other way. When you reach the number picked, leave the mouth open and have the person pick a color from the inside. Spell out the name of the color by opening the mouth first one way and then the other for each letter. Have the person pick another color. Lift the panel with their color on it and read them their fortune.

PENGUIN

In the wild, penguins live only in the Southern Hemisphere. These funny birds can't fly, but they can swim fast! This figure will look more lifelike if you make it out of paper that is a dark color on one side and light on the other.

1) Valley fold the paper in half diagonally and unfold.

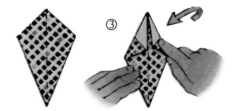

2) Valley fold both bottom sides so that they meet at the center crease.

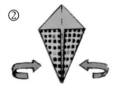

3) Turn the figure over. Valley fold both top edges so that they meet at the center crease.

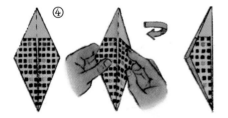

4) Turn the figure over again. Mountain fold the figure in half along the center line.

5) Valley fold the top layer of the figure to the left as shown to form a wing. Turn the figure over, form a wing on the other side, and turn the figure back over.

5) Form the duck's head by making another outside reverse fold.

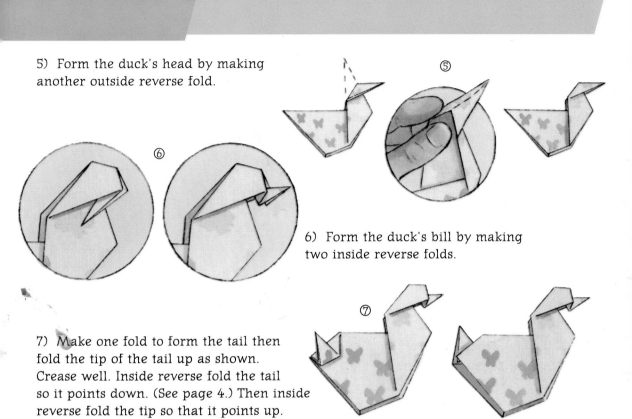

⑤

6) Form the duck's bill by making two inside reverse folds.

⑥

⑦

7) Make one fold to form the tail then fold the tip of the tail up as shown. Crease well. Inside reverse fold the tail so it points down. (See page 4.) Then inside reverse fold the tip so that it points up.

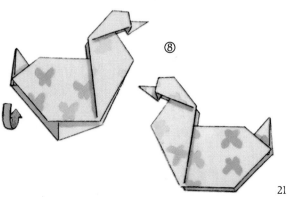

⑧

8) Mountain fold the bottom point so that it tucks inside as shown. Turn the figure over, mountain fold the other side, and your duck is done.

PETAL BOX

Keep tiny treasures in this little box. Make it out of special paper, and use it as a gift box.

1) Keep the color you want the box to be on the outside and valley fold the paper in half on the diagonal. With the long side of the triangle held away from you, valley fold the triangle in half.

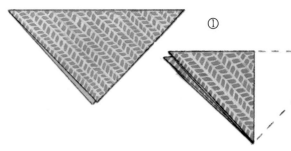

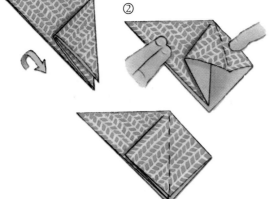

2) Squash fold the top layer of the figure. To do this, lift the top triangle and valley fold it back over itself. Unfold the crease you have just made. Put your fingers inside the top triangle, open it up, and flatten it so it forms a square. Turn the paper over, fold, and flatten the remaining triangle in the same way.

3) Make sure that the open ends of the paper are pointing down. Valley fold the top layer of both sides in to meet the center crease. The top layer of paper will now form a kite shape.

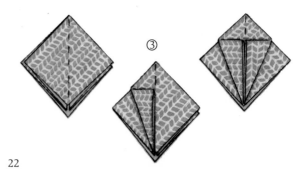

4) Open one side of the kite, slide a finger inside the two layers of paper, and flatten it into a smaller kite shape. Make sure that the center line on the top and bottom portion of the new kite line up. Do the same thing to the other side of the kite.

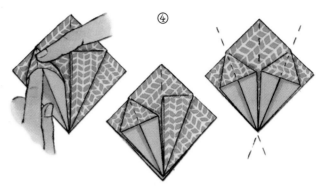

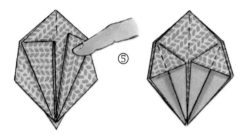

5) Turn the figure over and repeat Steps 3 and 4 on the other side.

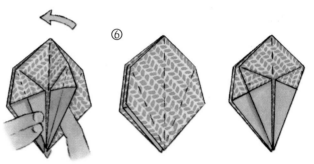

6) Fold the top layer of the right flap over to meet the left as if you were turning the page of a book. Valley fold the edges of the top layer to meet the center line.

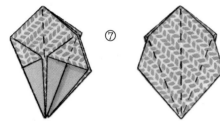

7) Turn the figure over. Fold the top right flap over to meet the left as you did in Step 6.

8) Valley fold the edges of the top layer to meet the center line as you did in Step 6.

9) To form the petals, valley fold the top layer of the bottom point up as far as you can. Turn the figure over and do the same on the other side. Fold the top right flap over to the left and fold the petal on this side up, too. Turn the flaps until you reach the last remaining point, and fold it up.

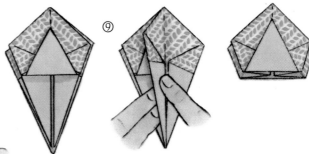

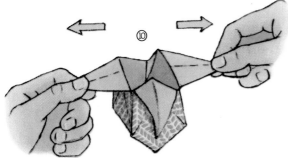

10) Hold the figure by the petals and gently pull it open. Put your fingers inside, turn the box over, flatten the bottom, and your petal box is ready to hold something special.

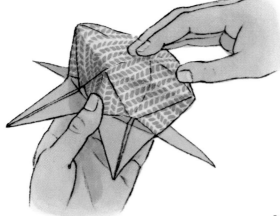

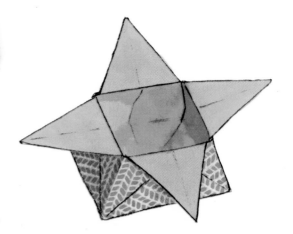

These inflatable boxes make great decorations. Glue them to a special gift or hang them from a tree.

1) Make a water bomb base. To do this, keep the color you want your box to be on the outside and valley fold the paper in half diagonally. Unfold the paper and valley fold the paper in half on the other diagonal. Crease well, then unfold the paper all the way.

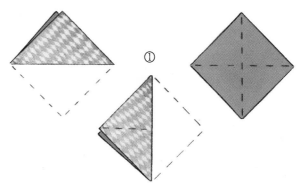

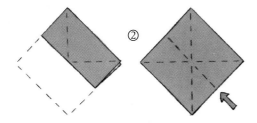

2) Mountain fold the paper in half, so it makes a rectangle, crease well and unfold.

3) Hold one end of the fold you made in Step 2 in each hand. Bring your hands together. Make sure the color you picked for the outside of the box is facing out. Carefully flatten the figure so that the fold from Step 2 is inside the figure and you have a triangle in the front and one in the back. This step completes the water bomb base.

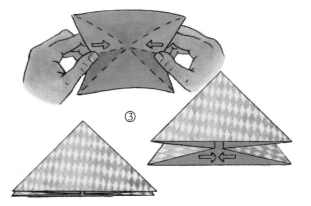

4) Valley fold the top layer of the two bottom points up to meet the top point. The top layer of the figure should now form a diamond shape.

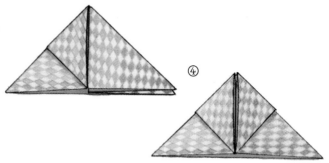

④

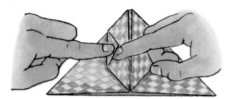

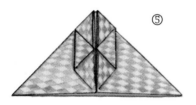

⑤

5) Valley fold both side corners of the diamond to meet in the center.

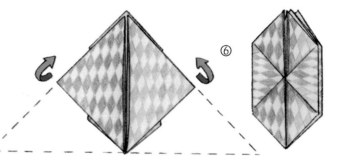

⑥

6) Turn the figure over and repeat Steps 4 and 5 on the other side.

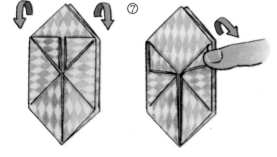

⑦

7) Valley fold the top layer of the two top points down so that they almost touch the corners that meet in the center. You will now have two small triangles on the top section of the figure. Valley fold the two small triangles along the lines formed by the center points. Crease well and unfold.

26

8) Lift the center points slightly. Put your finger inside the layers of paper and open the pockets. Tuck each small triangle into one of the pockets. Turn the figure over and repeat Steps 7 and 8 on the other side.

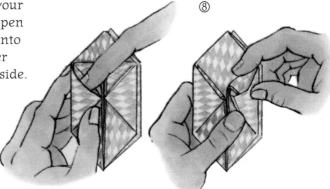

9) Make sure that all four triangles are tucked into a pocket. Hold the figure loosely by the bottom layer of paper. Blow hard into the hole and your balloon box will inflate!

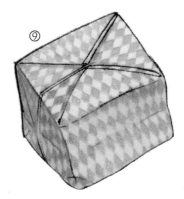

CLASSIC CRANE

The crane has been popular in Japanese art for centuries. It is considered a symbol of good luck and long life. Since World War II, origami cranes have come to represent the wish for peace throughout the world. For a serene atmosphere, make several of these cranes and hang them in your room.

1) Keep the color you want your crane to be on the outside. Valley fold the paper in half so it makes a triangle. With the long side held away from you, valley fold the triangle in half again.

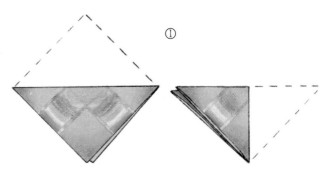

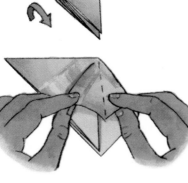

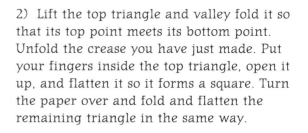

2) Lift the top triangle and valley fold it so that its top point meets its bottom point. Unfold the crease you have just made. Put your fingers inside the top triangle, open it up, and flatten it so it forms a square. Turn the paper over and fold and flatten the remaining triangle in the same way.

3) Make sure that the open ends of the paper are pointing down. Valley fold the top layer of both sides in to meet the center crease. You will now have a kite shape.

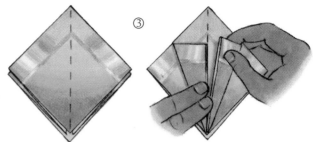

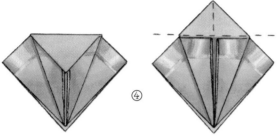

4) Valley fold the top point of the kite down as shown and crease well. Unfold the crease you have just made.

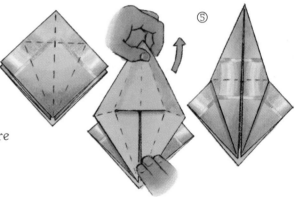

5) Open the sides of the kite by unfolding the flaps you made in Step 3. Lift the top layer of the kite's bottom point up so the paper bends at the crease you made in Step 4. Push the outside edges of the paper in to meet the center line. Then flatten the figure so that you have a long diamond shape.

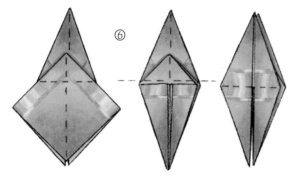

6) Turn the figure over and fold a kite shape on the remaining side as in Step 3. Repeat Steps 4 and 5 on this side. You will now have a two-sided long diamond. The bottom half of the diamond is split in two.

7) Valley fold the top layer of both bottom edges in to meet in the middle. Turn the figure over and repeat on the other side.

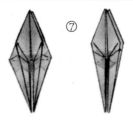

⑦

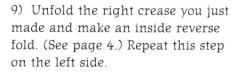

⑧

8) To make the crane's neck and tail, valley fold each half of the bottom section out to the sides as shown. Crease well.

⑨

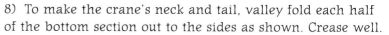

9) Unfold the right crease you just made and make an inside reverse fold. (See page 4.) Repeat this step on the left side.

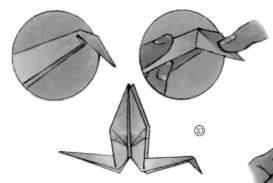

⑩

10) To form the head, fold down the end of the neck as shown. Unfold this crease and inside reverse fold the head.

11) Hold one of the crane's wings in each hand. Blow hard into the opening on the underside of the figure and gently separate your hands. Your crane will puff up and be ready to hang.

⑪

SEA TURTLE

Among the different species of sea turtle are the leatherback—the world's largest turtle—and the green turtle. The green turtle is often used to make soup. This figure is the most complex of all the figures in this book. Try it only after you have mastered several of the simpler figures.

1) Make a water bomb base. To do this, complete Steps 1-3 of the Balloon Box. Then do Step 4 of the Balloon Box.

2) Hold the point you just folded in place and valley fold the top edge of the left side to meet the center line. Repeat on the right side. Crease the folds well and unfold both points completely.

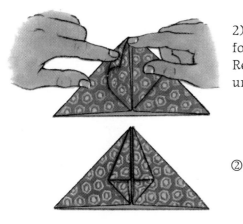

31

3) Here's the tricky part. The two points that make up the top and bottom layer on the left side are going to turn into the front legs. The points on the right will be the back legs. You are going to do different things to each side. First pinch the top point on the left so that it folds backward along its center crease. Push the top edge of the left side down toward the center line. Make the leg stand straight up in the air. Push the leg down so that its end meets the top point. You have now formed one of the front legs.

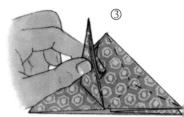

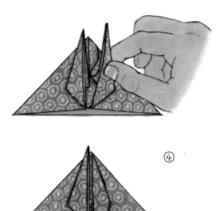

4) To make a back leg, pinch the top right point so it folds backward along its center crease. Push the top edge down toward the center line. Make the leg stand straight up in the air. Draw the end of the leg away from the top point and fold the leg so it points down.

5) Turn the figure over. Valley fold the left and right points up to meet the top. Crease well. Fold the top edges toward the center line. Crease well. Unfold the creases you have just made.

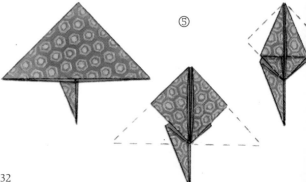

6) Since the back leg on the other side of the figure is now on the left, make another back leg on the left half of this side. Pinch the left point while pushing the top edge of the left side down so that the leg points straight up into the air. Fold the leg so that it points down.

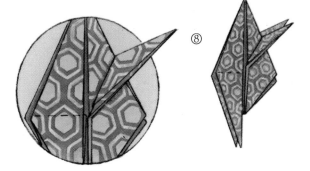

⑥

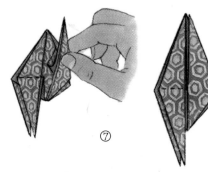

⑦

7) Now make a front leg on the right side. Pinch the point while pushing the top edge down to the center line. Push the leg down against the figure. Make sure that the legs on the left side of the figure are pointing down and that the ones on the right are pointing up.

8) Valley fold the front legs (the ones on the right) so they stick out to the right side as shown. You might want to match the angle of your fold to the angle of the fold in the drawing.

⑧

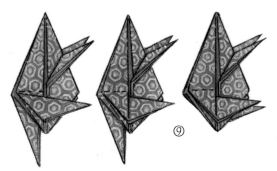

⑨

9) Inside reverse fold the back legs (the ones on the left) so that they point to the right.

33

10) Valley fold both back legs near the figure's center crease so that they stick out to the left. Then lift the whole right flap and fold it to the left as if you were turning the page of a book. Turn the figure over and lift the flap on the right and fold it to the left.

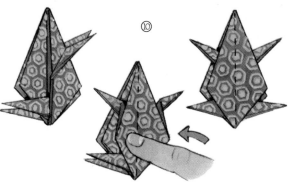

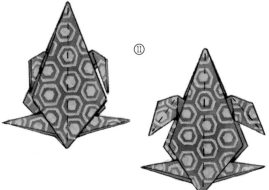

11) Fold the front legs down alongside the body. Crease well. Unfold the creases you have just made, separate the layers of paper that make up the front legs, and flatten the legs into flippers.

12) Fold the back legs as shown. You might need to open up the body of the turtle a little to do this. Crease well. Unfold the creases you have just made, separate the layers of paper, and flatten.

13) To form the neck and head, make a mountain fold near the front flippers. Then valley fold the head into place. If you want to, turn the figure over and fold the corners where the head joins the body to make the neck more lifelike.

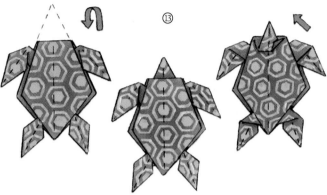

14) Fold the corners at the sides of the body underneath, and you have done the hardest figure in this book! Congratulations!

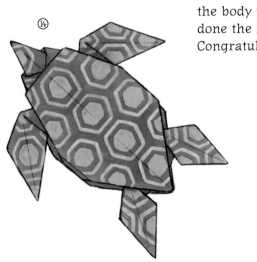

If you want to buy more origami paper, check your local craft or art supply stores. To order an origami catalog send a self-addressed business-size envelope with two first-class stamps to OrigamiUSA, Room CH-2, 15 West 77th Street, New York, NY 10024, or call (212) 769-5635.